Your Book of Badminton

The YOUR BOOK Series

Your Book of
Badminton

by
Len Wright

Hon. Secretary of the
English Schools' Badminton Association

FABER & FABER
3 Queen Square, London

First published in 1972
by Faber and Faber Limited
3 Queen Square London WC1
Printed in Great Britain by
Latimer Trend & Co Ltd Plymouth
All rights reserved

ISBN 0 571 09890 8

Contents

Illustrations

PHOTOGRAPHS

Illustrations

(Photographs by Alan Hall)

DIAGRAMS

Acknowledgements

Grateful thanks to Mr. A. Graves and Mr. F. Heywood for their encouragement; all the members of Kells School Badminton Club for their efforts; and Kathy and Janet Fife, Shona Stuart, Diane Hurst, Mickey Ruthery and Jimmy Kirkpatrick for their help with the photographs.

L.W.

Introduction

About eighteen years ago, a new secondary school was opened in Cumberland. The school was called Kells. It had a well-equipped gymnasium and a grand, spacious, high-ceilinged assembly hall. The P.E. programme included the usual games and activities for the winter and summer months, but it was decided to include a new activity suitable for a mixed group . . . badminton was chosen.

Interest was kindled by a few teachers playing the game at dinner-time and in the evenings. Soon the older pupils asked to join in, racquets and equipment were begged, borrowed and loaned, and after a very short time an enthusiastic group started a club, using the gym. Before long the numbers increased, a court was marked in the hall (it was quite a struggle to get permission) and with two courts to play on, the game's popularity increased in leaps and bounds. A school tuck-shop was started, and the profits helped to buy equipment for pupils who could not afford to buy their own—from friendly matches the team graduated to league games. Pupils left school but came back to play after work, often bringing boy friends or girl friends along. After a number of seasons the Club was fielding three league teams made up of staff, pupils, and old pupils. A tradition was being started and everybody was included—from the caretaker and cleaning staff, who allowed the pupils into school to play when most other schools had their doors closed, to the staff who coached and parents who ferried teams in their cars to fixtures.

Introduction

The Education Authority and School Governors were very generous in allowing free use of the facilities.

From little acorns big oak trees grow. The Club players filtered through to county teams; school teams were winning leagues; individuals were winning restricted and open tournaments; a group of pupils was formed into a 'Spotlight Team' and went about spreading the badminton gospel to other schools; the Cumberland Schools Badminton Association came into being and eventually led to the formation of the English Schools Badminton Association. One small group of especially talented youngsters, through hard work and dedication, between them won all the junior badminton championships in the country and one of the group went on to international honours.

Given help and encouragement from teachers and coaches, what the pupils from one school can do, pupils from other schools could do also.

I hope there is something for every young player in this book. If you haven't played before . . . how to start; for beginners . . . how to improve; for the school county player . . . some advanced subject matter; for the P.E. student . . . facts and figures which may help your P.E. thesis.

I

Why Play Badminton?

Badminton is slowly but surely pushing its way into the Physical Education timetable of many schools. Ten years ago badminton playing in school or even after school time was unheard of. Many young people were playing in local clubs and being coached by parents or interested club officials, but there was no national scheme to help them.

Five years ago, the English Schools' Badminton Association was formed by a group of teachers from Cumberland and Lancashire and from three counties, who were founder members, the Association has grown to a membership of twenty-six including Ulster and ranging from Cumberland in the north of England to Kent, Somerset and Cornwall in the south.

Today there are hundreds of schools and thousands of youngsters taking part in a full badminton playing programme which includes friendly inter-school games, school league matches, town and county tournaments for under 13's, under 14's, under 15's, under 16's and Open age, county matches and regional matches where teams are selected to play for the North, South and Midlands. Counties like Middlesex and Essex are sending school teams to play in Europe each year. The E.S.B.A. holds an inter-county competition each year, run on World Cup lines, and an Individual Tournament. Last year the first triangular international tournament was played in Dumfries—England *v.* Scotland *v.* Ireland under-16. Each county has its own coaching scheme for school players with its trained coaches and the aim is to make sure that everyone who wants help gets it, at school and when he leaves.

The E.S.B.A. works very closely with the Badminton Association of England (B.A. of E.), the body who is responsible for badminton in this country.

Why play badminton? Well, the first answer is that it is the up and coming game in schools, it is booming, and well-organized with opportunities for all age groups.

Badminton is an ideal sport for both boys and girls; hard work, good exercise with lots happening and great fun. Top class badminton play demands the agility of a gymnast, the endurance of a cross-country runner, the concentration of a chess player, and the determination of a rock climber. The game is played with a shuttlecock which can float gently like a parachute or fly at speeds up to 100 m.p.h. depending on how you hit it with the racquet. This variation of speed and flight makes badminton unique—it is not just another ball game. Matches are never rained off, so you can play all the year round, and when you leave school there is plenty of opportunity for you to go on playing. There are clubs in most towns and villages all over the country; clubs running two or three teams in leagues having as many as seven divisions; county teams with first, second and third teams; tournaments restricted to local players, or open tournaments where you can play against the best players in the country, or handicap matches where the not so good player could beat the best.

If you are really ambitious there is a good chance of playing for your country. Two young players, both playing school badminton only four years ago, are now playing for England. They are Ray Stevens (Essex) and Margaret Beck (Cumberland), while Barbara Giles (Essex), who played on her schools county team only three years ago, has been an England reserve. Mar-

1. Some well-known makes of racquets with feathered and plastic shuttlecocks

2. The Grip (backhand)

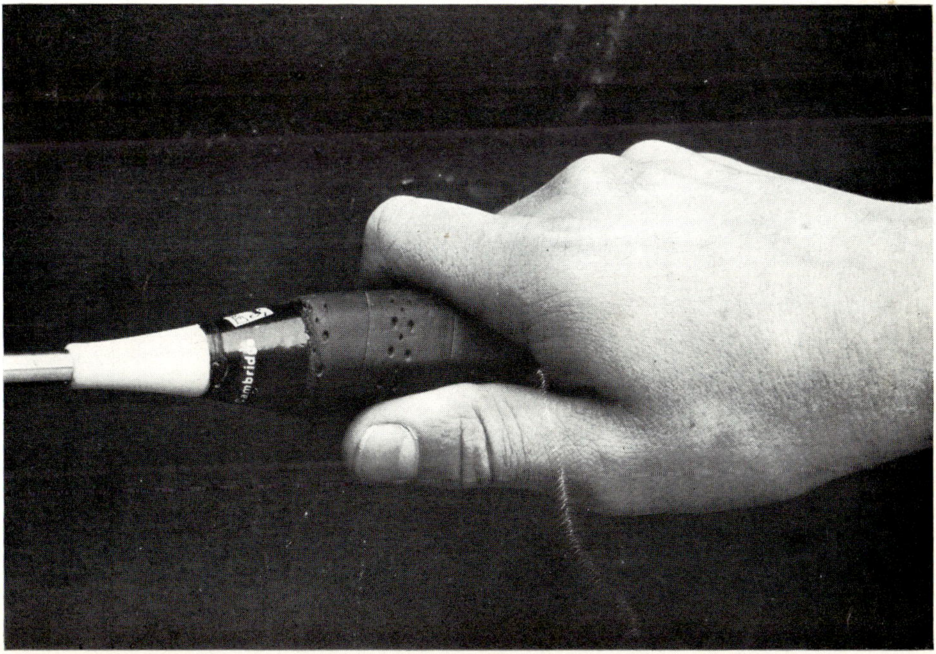

3. Hitting underhand on backhand
   side
4. Hitting overhead
5. Hitting overhead (backhand)

Why Play Badminton?

garet, now aged nineteen, is a seasoned campaigner who has been on trips to South Africa, Holland and Japan. She is a Gold Medallist from the last Commonwealth Games.

Although a new game to schools, badminton was played in this country as far back as the seventeenth century. In 1873 some army officers played the game in Gloucester at the home of the Duke of Beaufort—the place—Badminton! Gradually the game spread and in 1893 the B.A. of E. was formed. An English team went to Canada to play in 1925 and the Canadians took the game to the U.S.A. European countries started playing, especially Denmark. The game travelled to eastern countries through British travellers. The ruling body of world badminton is the International Badminton Federation formed in 1934. The most important international competitions are the Uber Cup for ladies' teams and the Thomas Cup for the men. The All-England Championships started in 1899 is recognized as the unofficial World Championship.

Why play badminton? It is a grand energetic game giving enjoyment and pleasure and demanding fitness and dedication. You can make yourself a good player through hard work; size and weight do not matter, and you are not too young to start at ten years old or too old at sixty. There are opportunities for personal progress at every level of ability and amenities are improving. AND you are wanted as a player—the more players we have the better the competition will be. We have taught many countries to play this game, but we have yet to win the Uber Cup or the Thomas Cup. You are needed to help put England on the top as a playing nation.

2

The Game of Badminton

Badminton may be played as a **Singles** game—one against one —or a **Doubles** game—two against two. Each player has a racquet to hit a **shuttlecock** over a net which is 5 feet high from the ground. The aim is to get the shuttle on to the ground on your opponent's side of the net. The playing area is a **court**. A singles court is 44 feet long by 17 feet wide, a doubles court is 3 feet wider. The two courts are marked out together, one on top of the other, so singles or doubles may be played. A shot or stroke is made when a player hits the shuttle with the racquet. Two players keeping the shuttle going over the net using strokes are playing a rally. You win a rally if you put the shuttle on the ground in your opponent's court or if you cause him to make an error (e.g. hit out of court or into the net). A mistake is usually called a fault.

The Singles Game

Imagine you are playing against friend Bill. You spin to decide who starts or serves first. You win, decide to serve first, and go to the right-hand service court. Bill goes to his right-hand receiving court which is diagonally across net. You serve, hitting shuttle over net with an underhand shot, and the rally starts. If you win the rally you get a point; lose, and Bill gets the serve and the chance to score. You can score points only if you have the service. When a point is won you cross over and serve from

Fig. 1. The Court: Two-in-One

(a) Short Service Line
(b) Doubles Long Service Line
(c) Singles Long Service Line

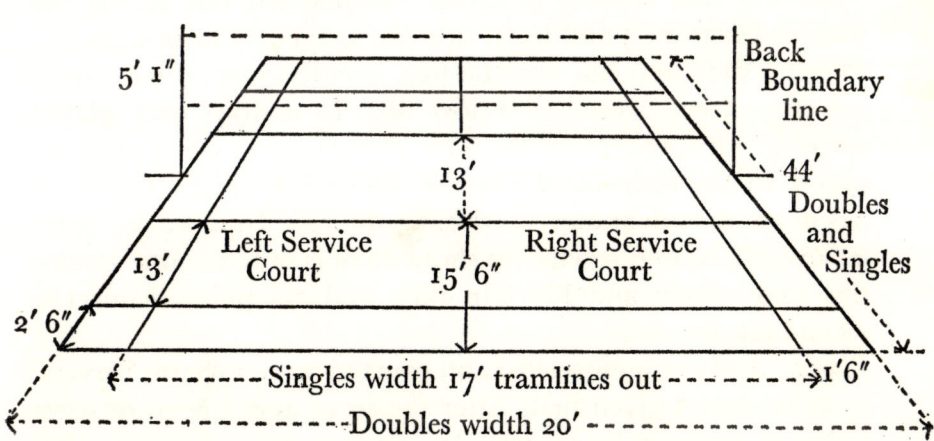

The Game of Badminton

the other service court, the receiver changes court also. After the service you may hit the shuttle to any part of court between net, side lines and back lines.

A game in men's singles and men's and ladies' doubles is usually 15 points; in ladies' singles 11 points. A match or **rubber** is three games, the winner being the player scoring most points in two out of three games.

Sometimes games are played to 21 points. In a 15 point game, if you and Bill tie at 13 points, whoever got 13 first may set (play the best out of 5 points). Setting may happen if the score is tied at 14 all (play the best of 3 points). In ladies' singles the game is set to 3 points at 9 all and to 2 points at 10 all.

The Doubles Game

This can be two boys playing two boys (men's or boys' doubles) or two girls playing two girls (girls' or ladies' doubles) or a boy and girl against a boy and a girl (mixed doubles). The serving and receiving courts are $2\frac{1}{2}$ feet shorter but $1\frac{1}{2}$ feet wider.

Serving and scoring is rather complicated but follow the plan in Diagram 3 and learn to score as quickly as you can.

Plan 1. Andy and Bill win the toss, decide to serve first. Andy serves to Tom. Score is 0–0 (love all). In doubles each player serves in turn, except at the start of each game when only the player in the right-hand court is allowed to serve. This is to cut down the advantage of winning the toss. Now we say score is 'love-all, second service' to show there is only the one service this time. Andy and Bill win rally and get point, score 1–0 second service and

Plan 2. Andy crosses to left-hand court to serve to Sam. Servers' score is always given first. After the serve and receipt of serve either player may hit shuttle. Andy serves, there is a rally, Bill hits shuttle into net, which is a fault, service is lost. No point

Fig. 2. Serving

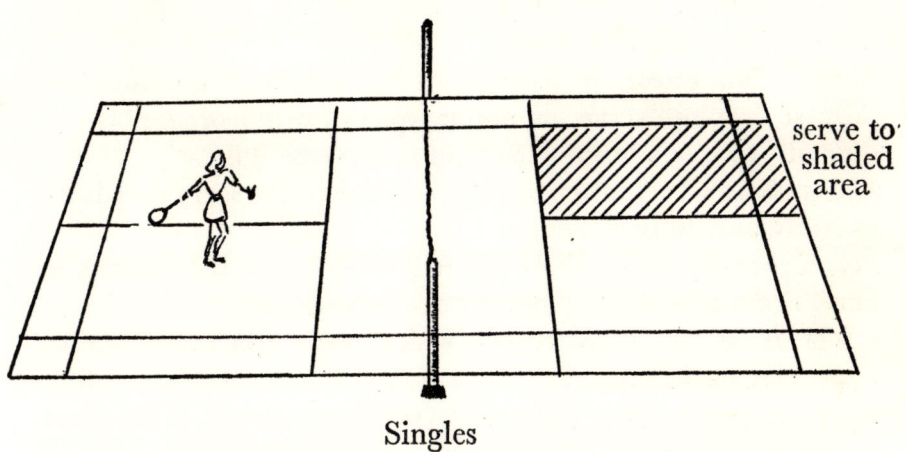

serve to
shaded
area

Singles

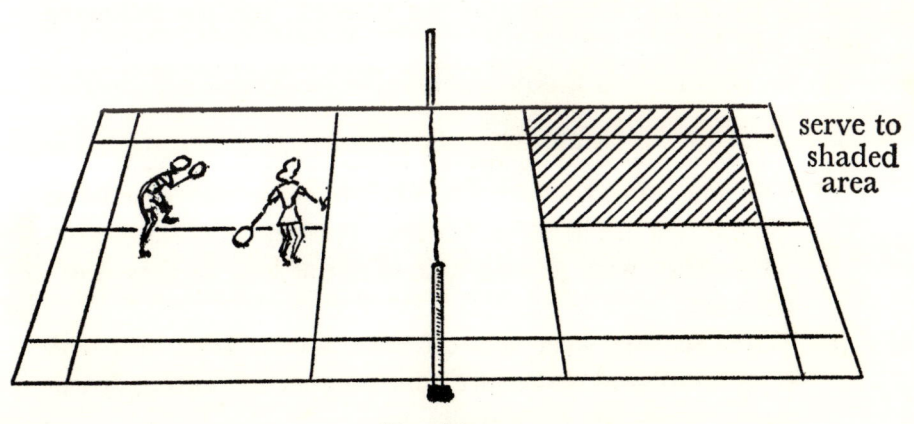

serve to
shaded
area

Doubles

The Game of Badminton

won or lost, just service changes to other side. Score is now
0–1 (love one) first service with Tom to serve to Bill since Tom
was in right-hand court to start.

Plan 3. Tom serves to Bill, Tom and Sam win next rally, score
now 1–1 (one all) first service.

Plan 4. Tom crosses to serve to Andy. Tom and Sam lose this
rally, so drop one serve (no points won or lost). Score is now 1–1
(one all) second service with Sam to serve to Bill.

Plan 5. Sam serves into net, rally is lost, and the serve goes back
to Andy and Bill.

Plan 6. Score now 1–1 (one all) first service with Bill to serve to
Sam. From now on all players get a serve in turn.

You must try to remember which court you should be in
when serving or receiving. In a doubles match fix your mind
where you were, left or right when the game started. If the score
is even you should be in same court as when the game began, if
uneven then court position reversed. In singles, serve is from
right-hand court when server's score even and left-hand court
when score is odd. This works for the receiver too. You must
swot up the rules of badminton for yourself, but the following
points will help:

(a) In doubles you should not receive two consecutive serves
in same game.
(b) Only the player being served to may return a service.
(c) You may stand where you wish to serve and receive as
long as you are in correct courts. Partners may stand anywhere they wish on own side of net as long as they don't
obstruct.
(d) When serving, keep feet off lines, always keep both feet
on ground, and make sure your racquet is pointing downwards when you hit shuttle.
(e) If you miss shuttle completely on serve have another go.
(f) A shuttle falling on line is in.

Fig. 3. Serving and Scoring

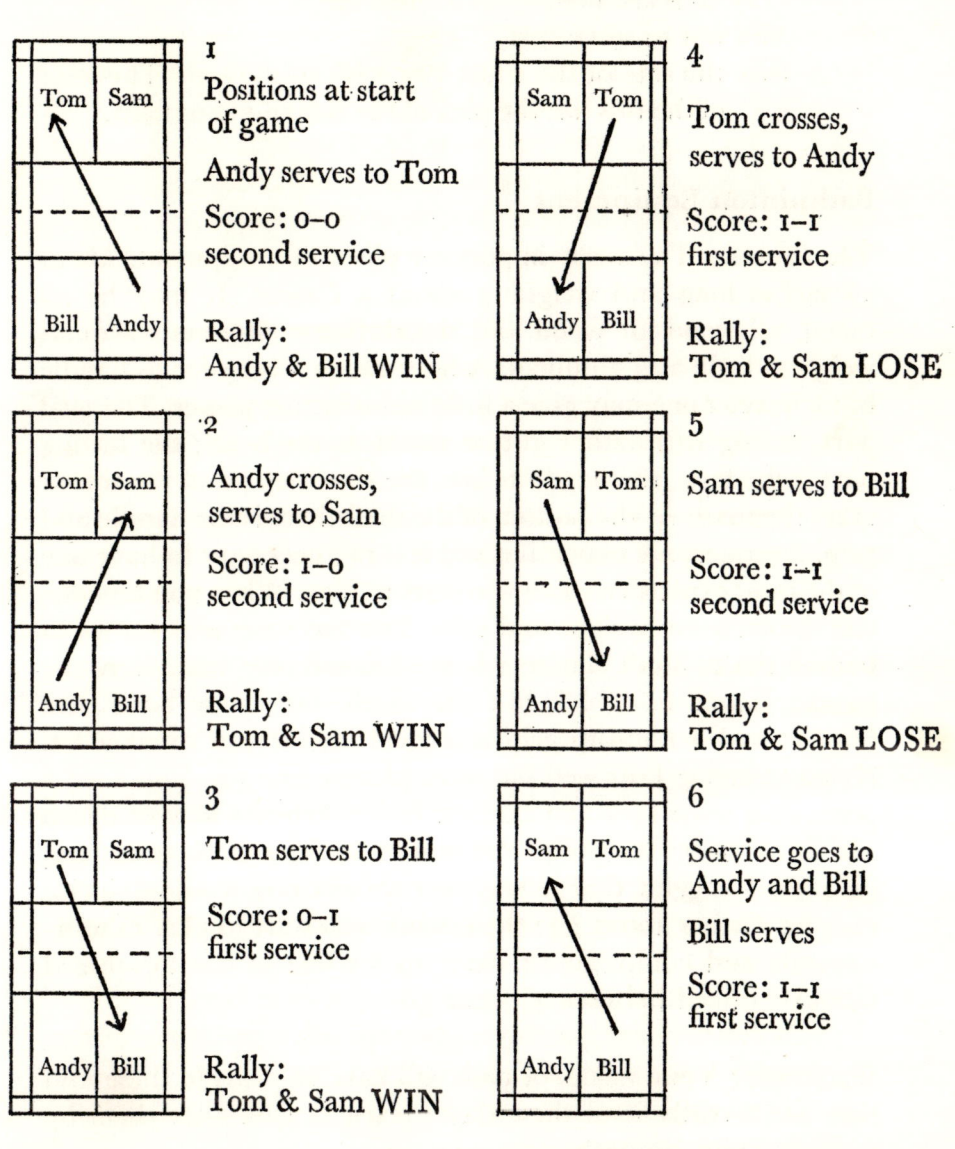

1

Positions at start of game

Andy serves to Tom

Score: 0–0
second service

Rally:
Andy & Bill WIN

2

Andy crosses,
serves to Sam

Score: 1–0
second service

Rally:
Tom & Sam WIN

3

Tom serves to Bill

Score: 0–1
first service

Rally:
Tom & Sam WIN

4

Tom crosses,
serves to Andy

Score: 1–1
first service

Rally:
Tom & Sam LOSE

5

Sam serves to Bill

Score: 1–1
second service

Rally:
Tom & Sam LOSE

6

Service goes to
Andy and Bill

Bill serves

Score: 1–1
first service

(g) If you win the toss you may choose one of the following:
   (i) to serve first,
   (ii) not to serve first,
   (iii) the side of the court you wish to start on. The loser of the toss has the pick of the remaining options.

Badminton Equipment

The Racquet: The most important piece of equipment, about 26 inches long and weighing about 5 ounces. It may be all metal, all wood, or wood and metal. Some all-metal racquets weigh as little as 3·7 ounces. A light racquet is easier to handle but a heavier one may give a little more hitting power. The oval part, strung with either gut or nylon, is the head; the hitting part is the face; the head fits into the shoulders; and the throat takes the shaft. At the bottom of the shaft there is the handle and grip. Racquets are expensive and it is not necessary to have one of the most expensive when you start to play. When you buy one test the balance, weight and grip. You use your wrists a lot in badminton so don't choose a heavy-headed one; make sure the handle is not too thick but fits nicely into your hand and fingers; and a non-slip grip is a good idea if you sweat a lot. Nylon stringing lasts well but most players like gut. You need a press, and must keep the racquet in it when not in use: damp and heat cause warping. Put your name on both press and racquet. I suggest that a beginner should buy a middle-price racquet costing about £4; then, when you start to play in tournaments and competitions, save up for one of the top-priced racquets priced between £7 and £8.

Shuttlecocks: Your school or club will have to provide these and they are a costly item these days; learn to look after them by treating them properly.

The Game of Badminton

There are two kinds—feathered and plastic.

Feathered shuttles are used in all top-class senior games. They have a cork base covered with kid and goose feathers are glued into the base. It is said that it takes one goose to make a shuttle. There is a small weight in the base. The feathers are easily damaged and a broken feather or a cut base spoils the flight. The speed is governed by the weight of the shuttle measured in grains, and weights vary from about 77 to 83 grains: 80 grains is the medium speed and in most common use. The size and temperature of a hall does affect the speed; the warmer the room the faster the shuttle flies.

Nowadays most schools and practically all school tournaments use plastic shuttles. They are cheaper, last longer and are easier to get. The firm making them have done much experimenting trying to get their shuttle to fly like the feathered one. The plastic shuttle has a nylon skirt which is fitted into a rubber base. They are sold in three colours which indicate the shuttle speed —red is fast, blue is medium, and green is slow.

Prices: Feathered, from about 12p to 25p each.

Plastic, from 9p to 15p.

Shuttles last longer when treated kindly; never hit them along the floor or scoop them up with the racquet. Feathers should be smoothed out between fingers now and again, and kept in a cool damp place.

Clothes for Badminton: While you are a beginner and learning I would suggest you use your usual P.E. kit. I believe it is more important to have a racquet than to spend money on special clothing. When you are playing in matches or taking part in tournaments you must wear white—shirts, blouses, shorts, skirts, socks and gym shoes. A track suit is very useful. Be particular about the type of gym shoe you buy. Many young players use the cross-country running shoe which is ideal for concrete floors

25

but a little too heavy for the ordinary wooden floor. You need a light shoe with a soft sorbo underfoot padding. Some gym shoes have reinforced uppers which prevent wearing on the outside.

Unfortunately it is rather an expense to get kitted out for badminton, but don't be put off. Don't worry if you can't afford everything at once; get the most important things first and build up gradually. Get a racquet first, or if the school supply them don't be too proud to learn with that until you can afford your own.

Get started to play any way you can—that is the most important thing. A number of top class players have started their careers with old racquets which have been given to them.

3

Starting to Play Badminton

Hitting the Shuttle for the First Time

This exercise is to get you used to hitting a shuttle and to control the flight. Hold your racquet as though shaking hands with it, get the shuttle in your other hand, drop it floorwards, then with a good underhand shot hit shuttle up to ceiling. Keep on hitting it and keep your eye on it all the time. At first you will be running all over the court to get under the shuttle as it comes down, but after a minute or two you will be able to stand in one spot and keep the shuttle going up and down. Then vary the height, a low hit then a high one. Now check your grip and make sure you are still shaking hands with it; look at the V between the thumb and forefinger; make sure there is only about half an inch of racquet sticking out beyond your hand and don't grip too tightly; use your fingers, not the palm; all the grip should be with first finger and thumb. You can check the grip by holding the racquet in your left hand and sliding your flat hand, with fingers spread out, from strings to grip. When fingers of right hand meet the handle stop about half-inch from bottom and wrap fingers round the grip. **Check your grip frequently when you start to play: it affects the way the racquet is swung. You can't play good strokes with a faulty grip. If it feels unnatural at first, have patience**

27

and persevere. You can play all the shots in badminton with this grip.

Underhand and Overhead Shots

This is usually a group practice with a dozen pupils hitting to each other across the court from side line to side line. Should there be only two then play the length of the court and over the net. First stand sideways to net with left shoulder and left foot pointing to it (N.B. right-handed player), have racquet pointing downwards to floor, allow shuttle to drop from waist high out of other hand and with a good underhand swing hit shuttle over net from just below waist high. With a partner or coach on other side of net you keep shuttle going to each other. To bring in overhead shots hit shuttle extra high, don't allow it to drop, and with racquet held well above your head hit the shuttle at a point about 2 feet above head height. Keep hitting above net to partner. Remember to stay sideways on, pointing shoulder in direction you want shuttle to go, hit with a straight arm, and keep racquet face square to shuttle. The more time you spend on this exercise the better your shots will be. Aim to develop an easy flowing action, a good long swing and hit the shuttle as early as you can. Gradually increase the power of your overhead shots without losing direction until you can hit a good length. Play long rallies, count the number of times you can hit without the shuttle going on the floor and when you are fairly good make each other run about the court; aim to put the shuttle out of your partner's reach.

Remember to:
(a) Check grip.
(b) Watch shuttle on to your racquet.
(c) Go to meet shuttle, catch it early, hit with a straight arm, try not to bend elbow.

(d) Keep sideways on; badminton, like cricket, is a game played sideways.

(e) Keep far enough away from shuttle to get a good swing at it.

(f) Face of racquet should be square with shuttle when hitting.

Backhand: When a player plays a stroke to a shuttle on his right side (right-handed player) we call this the forehand side, when the shuttle is hit from the left side this is called the backhand side. It is more difficult to make shots on this side. Practise by standing square to net, swing your racquet across the body, at the same time move your right leg across too. Your right shoulder and quite a bit of your back should now be pointing to net, relax at the knees and dip into the shuttle as you hit it. You use the opposite side of playing surface of racquet face to hit with and connect with shuttle about waist high. It helps if you put your thumb flat and straight along the bevel of handle and tilt racquet slightly to shuttle. The more time you spend practising this shot, both underhand and overhead, the less of a bugbear it will be later on. You can learn the correct swing and rhythm by grooving or shadowing the shot (i.e. playing without the shuttle, just imagining it is there). Remember to turn opposite side to all backhand shots; use opposite foot forward; keep well away from shuttle to let yourself get a good swing, and keep your elbow pointed at the shuttle.

You will need many nights of practice just hitting the shuttle over the net before you start thinking of playing a game. If you can't keep the shuttle in play, the rallies are too short and you get fed up. Hours spent on stroke technique are never wasted. The ability to play good shots is all important—you can't place the shuttle where you want to unless you hit it properly.

A Few Tips About Stroke Playing

Give yourself as much time as possible to play shot by getting to shuttle quickly.

Get your feet right; then you will be in correct position.

Don't grip racquet too tightly.

In overhead shots action is similar to throwing a javelin or cricket ball; in underhand shots it is like throwing underhand. When playing overhead point left arm to shuttle, take racquet up between shoulder-blades (scratch your back with it), elbow bent, wrist cocked (i.e. bent back), reach up to shuttle straightening arm and wrist and racquet till all in line, then just before you hit shuttle straighten wrist.

Keep eye on shuttle and hit through it.

Point of impact (spot you hit shuttle) is in front of your head just about in line with your front foot.

Body weight goes into shot by swopping weight from back foot to front; then follow through with racquet along shuttle line.

The Serve: A most important shot . . . the shot to start a game. Serve may be low (i.e. just clearing net to land on opponent's front service line) or high to arrive at back of opponent's service court. In doubles serve from a spot about 18 inches from front service line and 12 inches from middle line. For singles stand farther back, 3 to 4 feet behind front service line. Remember you have different areas to serve to in doubles and singles. The low serve is used most often in doubles, the high one in singles.

Low Serve: Take up position, take your time, concentrate on what you are trying to do. Keep shuttle as low as possible over net and drop it on, or just behind, opposite service line. Drop shuttle from about waist high, swing racquet forward keeping

30

its head pointed to ground and wrist cocked, connect with shuttle in front of left knee and gently push shuttle over net keeping wrist cocked. Cocked wrist helps keep shuttle low. While hitting let your weight ease forward on to the front foot. Aim shuttle at centre of opponent's T junction and watch it all the time.

High Doubles Serve: Stance is the same as for low serve and action is very similar except you need a little more push to get shuttle over opponent's racquet and to back of his court. Wrist is uncocked at impact; follow through to get extra length.

High Singles Serve: Needs a lot more punch to get as much height as possible and shuttle to back line. Point of impact is well in front of server and shuttle pushed away so that greatest height is at back of court and not above net. This is usual serve in singles.

Receiving the Serve (doubles): Adopt the 'ready position', that is front foot about 12 inches from front service line. Lean forward towards net with racquet held above net, be poised on toes ready to move forward quickly to take shuttle coming over net or to get back to a high serve. When receiving in right-hand court be about 2 feet from centre line but in left-hand court 3 or 4 feet so you can use your forehand. When receiving in singles, stance should be farther back from front service line since most serves will be high. You should try to get the shuttle on the floor at every opportunity when playing. Hit down and attack; if you hit the shuttle upwards you are losing the attack and defending. Your serve and receipt of serve will decide your play in a rally, whether you defend or attack.

A good low service gives you a chance to attack in doubles; a high service gives your opponent the chance. When you receive

Fig. 4. Flight of Shuttlecock

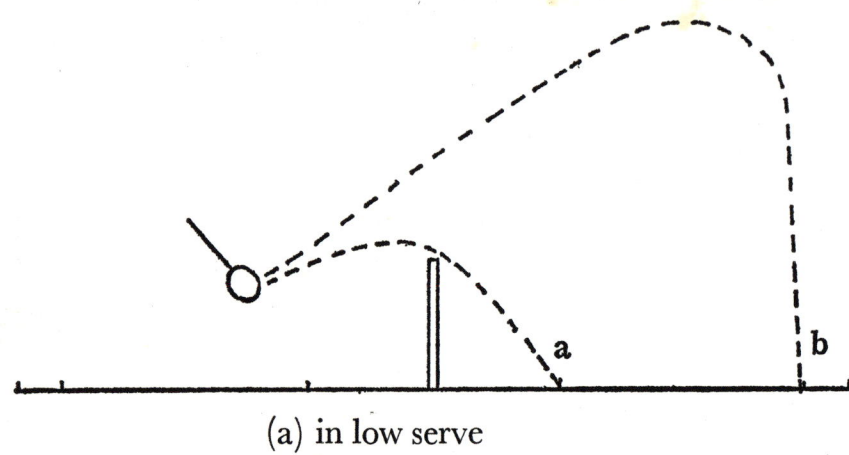

(a) in low serve
(b) in high doubles serve

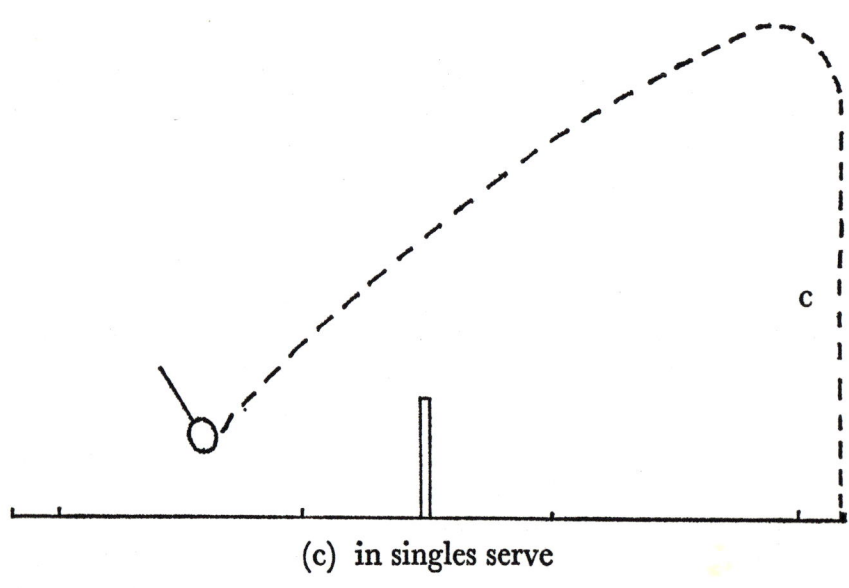

(c) in singles serve

6. Ready position. Preparing to serve
7. Low serve. Very little follow through
8. High singles serve showing cocked wrist

9. High singles serve showing follow-through
10. Finish of high singles serve
11. Receiving the serve, "ready position"

a high service it should be hit down or attacked. In singles you serve high to make it harder for the opposition at the back of the court to attack and to start him running.

Once you can serve and receive, there are four shots to be learned and mastered which are the backbone of the game. They are played on the forehand and backhand sides and their technique and use must be fully understood.

The Smash: Your most important point-winning shot. It puts the shuttle into the other court as soon, as fast and as steeply as possible. It is a power shot—the racquet head travels very fast, body, arm and wrist all combining to give full power. Shuttle is taken as high and early as possible; hit it ahead of your body about 18 inches in front of right shoulder then follow through along line of flight past the legs. Use the smash when the shuttle is put up to you at net or anywhere in the front three-quarters of your court.

The Clear or Lob: Mainly a defensive stroke. Shuttle is cleared to back of opponent's court if you are in difficulty in a rally and you want time to stop his attack. Hit the full length of court and as high as possible; a short clear gives the chance to smash. Shot can be underhand or overhead, and hit so that greatest height is at back of court. Left foot pointing to net, body sideways, left shoulder to net, good backswing, racquet going up and over shoulder, wrist cocked, elbow bent, swing forward straightening arm and wrist to hit shuttle with body weight going into shot. Point of impact about in line with front shoulder; 'throwing' action is used and shuttle is hit up and away from you. The clear is used a lot in singles but over used in doubles.

The Drop Shot: This stroke 'drops' the shuttle into your opponent's front court and as near to the net as possible. Since the shuttle is going down it is an attacking shot, and it can be played from anywhere in your own court underhand or overhead. The power is less than the smash so shuttle travels slower. There are two types of drop. The slow or floating used in singles, played from back of court when your opponent is at the back of his court but never used in doubles, and the fast drop which is a kind of semi-smash, more powerful than the floater so it lands farther away from net. It is a handy shot in doubles, for turning defence into attack (i.e. picking up a smash) or for putting shuttle down in open spaces. Action similar to that used for smash (overhead drop); in fact you should learn to hit the drop with the same body swing as for smash, but slow down shuttle speed at last possible second so your opponent will be deceived. Don't drop when you can smash.

The Drive: Another attacking shot, really a smash played sideways from waist height. Used mainly in mixed doubles by man, who meets shuttle half-court, chest high and hits flat and fast so that shuttle just clears net travelling parallel to floor. Because shot is usually played from side lines with man stretching, footwork is very important, short sharp steps to get there with a longer step before hitting from either left or right foot whichever is easiest (forehand drive). With toes pointing to side line, bring racquet head up and behind back shoulder with wrist cocked and elbow bent, swing shoulders and hips forward towards net, and take racquet round in a good wide arc, body weight on front foot. Then straighten arm and uncock wrist to connect with shuttle just in front of leading foot, following through across body, turning racquet face to floor and rolling wrist on top.

Although it is better for the beginner to hit the forehand drive over the left leg, good players play the shot off either foot. For

Fig. 5. Flight of Shuttlecock

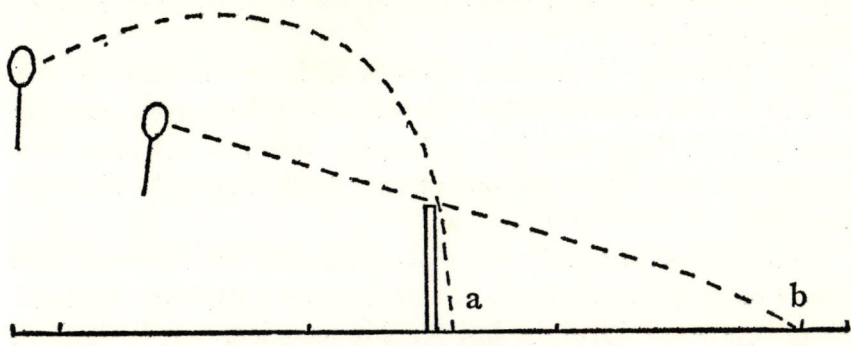

(a) in slow drop shot
(b) in smash from half-court

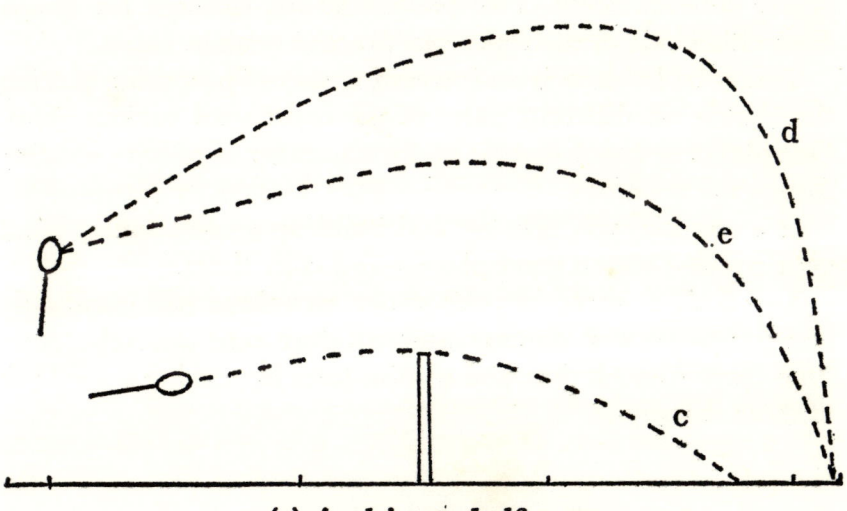

(c) in drive to half-court
(d) in clear (defensive)
(e) in clear (attacking)

the backhand drive you must hit over your right leg, i.e. point right toe to side lines, don't crowd the shuttle, give yourself room to swing.

The best way to practise shots is to have someone hit the shuttle to you from the other side of the net. You need someone who can put the shuttle just in the right spot for each shot, preferably a coach. You can perfect your stroke action by shadowing shots.

Playing against a wall with a plastic shuttle helps serving, and many other shots, and you can throw the shuttle for yourself. Gym beams are ideal for low serving practice. Set the bottom one for net and use the top one as a guide about 12 inches above, gradually lowering it as you get better.

Two high jump stands and a bar can be used as a net for serving practice. Six ropes hanging from a gym roof have five spaces between them. Two players hitting through the spaces from either side of the ropes can practise straight clears.

Target badminton is an interesting way of practising placing the shuttle on different parts of the court with various shots. One player or coach can hit up for a number of players wanting to practise accuracy.

It is essential you practise and build up a good action in all your strokes; watch good players and copy them.

Any fault or error in your stroke technique will eventually cost you points and matches, and will have to be put right sometime. Save yourself time and trouble later by making a good job of those shots now.

4

Elementary Badminton

You have learnt all the strokes necessary for playing a game and you now have to learn the tactics required to beat your opponents.

Singles

This is the best game for learning strokes and how to play them on the move. The basic tactics are simple: you run your opponent around the court, putting the shuttle where he isn't, hoping he won't be able to get to it, or at least that he will make a mistake or give you the chance of an easy smash for a winner. The singles court is long and narrow, and you use the long and short shots—high serve, clear, drop, and wait for a chance to smash. If your opponent has gone to his back line you play a drop shot near the net to make him run, if he is near the net then you play a clear to make him run back. You try your best to run the opposition around the court by making him run along the diagonals, for instance, forehand corner on back line to backhand corner at net. All your shots must be accurate—long, deep clears right on back line (and high serves) with drop shots very close to net. Accurate drops and clears could make your opponent travel about 22 feet to play two strokes, but if your clear or service is a yard short and your drop is another yard over the net he has 6 feet less to run. In a long singles match this would add up to a lot of feet and could mean you tiring first.

Elementary Badminton

The main serve is the high one, the short one used now and again for surprise, and don't waste energy by too much smashing but wait for the winner (e.g. bad high serve or short clear, poor net shot.) As you know serving and receiving positions are 3 to 5 feet back from front service line and for serving—about 18 inches from centre line. For receiving stand a little farther back, about 2½ feet. After serving and receiving, players should make a base on centre line close to and in line with where they served from, and they move back to this base after playing each shot. This saves you a lot of extra running and helps you move around court smoothly since it is the shortest distance from all spots on the court. Later you will learn how to change this base to meet different conditions of play.

Answer clears with clears and drop shots with underhand lobs; be accurate; look for your opponent's weaknesses (often backhand corner) and attack them; keep the shuttle in play, chase everything giving few points away (this is called playing tight); and play steadily . . . concentrate . . . think!

Doubles

This is a team game and you play for each other by working together to score points; it doesn't matter who gets the winner so long as it is your team. Two individuals playing their own games will be murdered by a good team on the other side.

To work as a team you must know where you should be at certain times during the game—and where your partner is. You must know the best shot to play in any situation to give the pair of you the best chance of winning points, and you have to back each other up to cover all the gaps on court in order to stop the opposition scoring. In any badminton game hitting the shuttle up towards the ceiling puts you on the defensive; and if you hit the shuttle down towards the floor you are attacking. The player or players attacking most in any game has the better chance of winning. **In doubles your main idea should be to hit down (i.e. attack) at every opportunity.**

Men's and Ladies' Doubles (Boys'/Girls' Doubles)

Tactics similar for both games but men's doubles is usually much faster with more smashing. It is a fact the best formation for attack is to play 'back and front', that is one partner looking after about one-third of the court nearest net the other looking after the back two-thirds. The player at the net deals with all shuttles just clearing the net, the one behind looks after the higher shuttles, both players doing their best to hit down. Usually the back player smashes and plays the shots for his partner to get a chance of finishing the rally at the net, or the net player pushes and probes trying to get the opposition to put a high shuttle up for his partner behind to smash a winner.

It is also a fact that the best defensive formation is to play 'sides'. This means each player looks after half the court from the net to the back line. He has less court to cover since he only takes shot in his own half and there is less chance of gaps being left. Pairs don't attack or defend all the time so you have to learn how to move from one position to the other.

In a doubles game both pairs start off in attacking positions, i.e. 'back and front'. Should the server serve low (shuttle kept low so attacking) he moves in to net with racquet up, prepared to play at net while his partner looks after back two-thirds of court. They stay like that while both are hitting down. If the receiver plays the shuttle down over net (again attacking) then that pair assume attacking formation. Sooner or later one pair will have to give way and defend, imagine one player at the back is being run around, he wants help or he will lose the point . . . he hits the shuttle up to the other back line, his partner comes back from net and they play sides. As soon as they get a chance to attack or hit down, then they move to back and front positions again, either the one hitting down goes to net or the one nearest. The other partner moves back to centre line again. There are some basic moves which become automatic with practice. Should you decide to serve high then you drop back to 'sides'. When receiving—if you are high served to, then as you go back to hit, your partner moves forward to cover net. When playing sides you move opposite from your partner, just as if you were connected together by a rod. Should your partner move two steps towards net to play a shot then you take two steps back to cover the gap. It is essential both players keep moving whether or not they hit the shuttle. Remember you move from attack to defence and vice versa on your own shots not the opposition's shots!

When attacking against a pair playing sides or defensive—attack between them, down the middle of the court and at the net, a pair playing back and front are most vulnerable on the side lines.

Mixed Doubles

Usually the girl plays at the net and the boy looks after the back two-thirds of the court, an attacking formation. The man smashes and drives at the opposition trying to find an opening or get a poor return at the net for his partner to kill. The girl must be on her toes and ready to move to finish off any rally. She plays on or about the front service line with her racquet held up at net height, willing and ready to take the shuttle as soon as it crosses the net. She must try not to hit up and avoid hitting the shuttle to the opposite boy's racquet to give him an easy shot. With the girl playing at the net and the boy having a lot of court to cover it is very important that the opposition are not allowed to attack; they must be denied the attack for as long as possible.

A frequently used tactic in mixed doubles is a high serve to the girl to force her back and away from the net, the answer is to smash when you can, play a fast drop away from the other girl, or if in real trouble, clear high and deep to opposite back line and get back to net to cover.

During a game partners may be drawn out of position . . . the boy may have to help at the net or the girl drop back to sides if the boy is being run around on the back line and is losing. When this happens the return shot played should be one that gives you and your partner as much time as possible to get back to your normal positions, unless you can win the point playing sides. If the girl gets stuck on the back line she will be weakening her team's chances of winning unless she is a very strong player.

Net Play

Playing at net is a very essential part of doubles teamwork and often neglected. Badminton matches, especially doubles, are won at the net and here are a few hints which will be helpful:

(a) Take every opportunity of going into net; try to dominate; learn to be a 'tiger'.

(b) Keep racquet up always; be on your toes ready to move either way; eyes front.

(c) Don't get too close to net; heels on front service line; go in to net to play shot; dab shuttle down on to floor; then back to base again ready for next shot.

(d) Take shuttle as early as possible; use wrists, if you have to play shuttle below net don't let it drop lower than you need and try to play a close accurate net return back; if this is not possible keep shuttle away from opponent at net; don't present a chance for easy smash; lob to back line.

Doubles Teamwork

A few essentials which will help your doubles teamwork. Practise serving low: a good low serve is a basic necessity. Change the angle of your serve now and again. Learn and practise attacking a serve; move towards it pushing shuttle on to ground, or into server's body, or to half court side lines. Don't hit up unless you have to and not too many high serves. If you have to clear make it deep and to back line, don't give opposition chance of an easy smash through short clearing. **Play as a team and for each other.**

5

Advanced Badminton

Once you have mastered stroke technique and the basic tactics of badminton, the standard of your game will improve. It will also become very evident that there is a lot more to this game than just hitting a shuttle over a net and hoping for the best. You will realize you have to use your brain and think, and because badminton is played at such a fast pace you must learn to think very quickly.

The good player is very proficient in his strokes so that he can put the shuttle where he wants it at any time in the game. He is able to move across the court quickly, get to the shuttle early and give himself as much time as possible to play his shots. He is fit so that he can keep on moving for a long time, and he must be able to think out the correct tactics and strategy to force his opponent to make mistakes or give chances for winners. You must work out your own game against every opponent or pair. Think out the ways you are going to break down his or their game and answer any tactics used against you. Each shot is significant in your overall strategy. In badminton it is not always the better player who wins, often it is the better tactician, the thinker, and the player with the guts to stick to a plan and keep going.

Learn to concentrate while you are playing, and ignore what is happening outside the court. One of the best ways of doing this is to watch the shuttle. In cricket a good batsman watches the ball as soon as the bowler starts his run up; you watch the shuttle as soon as it is picked up to serve. Don't hit the shuttle to any old spot on court, but have in mind just where you are going to hit it and why. Aim at a spot, keep the shuttle in play, be mean, don't give away points needlessly.

Try to diagnose the opposition's game and find out the weaknesses. Are they fast or slow around the court? Do they like to attack or defend? How powerful is the smash? Do they leave the net open? What is the backhand like? Do they tire after long rallies? Once you have found out the weakness, exploit it and win the match as quickly as you can.

Most important of all, know your own game and try to cut out any weakness so that it can't be attacked. If your backhand is poor, practise until it is good; make sure your serve is good; if your smash is not powerful make sure it is accurate. Never let your feelings show in a game; if you get decisions against you don't lose your temper.

Some players are defensive-minded, others like to attack; you should build both attitudes into your game. If you are a defender don't ignore the chance to attack when it comes, there is nothing wrong in being patient and waiting for a point. If it is your nature to attack don't go blasting away at the shuttle losing more points than you win just for the sake of attacking, but learn to attack sensibly, recognizing when you have a good defender against you. You must be prepared to change your tactics when the occasion demands. Avoid playing the type of game your opponent wants you to play and don't allow your game to become predictable and stereotyped. Don't go on court prepared to be a good loser—go on determined to win whatever the opposition, but always remembering that it is possible to be a determined winner and a good sport. If you do lose make the winner fight for every point and lose in a sporting manner.

Advanced Singles

You already know that (a) you should try to run your opponent as much as possible over the court; (b) good length clears and accurate drops are essential; and (c) the main serve is the high one. The smash is used when there is the chance of a winner, and in the modern game its use is increasing with players using the smash to create openings.

A high serve or clear falling at right angles to the back line is difficult to smash and is easily picked up and played as an underhand drop shot at the net. This will bring the smasher running from the back to the net, so **good length is a must for the singles player.**

Make your opponent run along the court diagonals, the longest distances, by playing shots to the four corners.

The high serve is used most but the low serve may be used at times as a surprise and to catch an opponent on the wrong foot if they start moving back too early to hit your high serve. Your high serve should be varied in height and direction, the 'lower' high serve gives players less time to get back with the result that they have more chance of hitting a bad return. Direction of serve should be varied between junction of centre line and back line and junction of side line and back line. When shuttle is served to outer line, players often do not get far enough back and their return is short. This serve also makes them run farther if the next shot is a drop over net to opposite side of court. Should your opponent expect a short service and go forward to attack, then the shuttle is flicked over his head and racquet to the back of the court. This **flick serve** is used often in doubles to make players think twice about attacking the low serve.

When playing singles keep on the move all the time, getting back to base after each shot. Should you be caught well out of

Fig. 6. Variations of Serve and Angles of Return

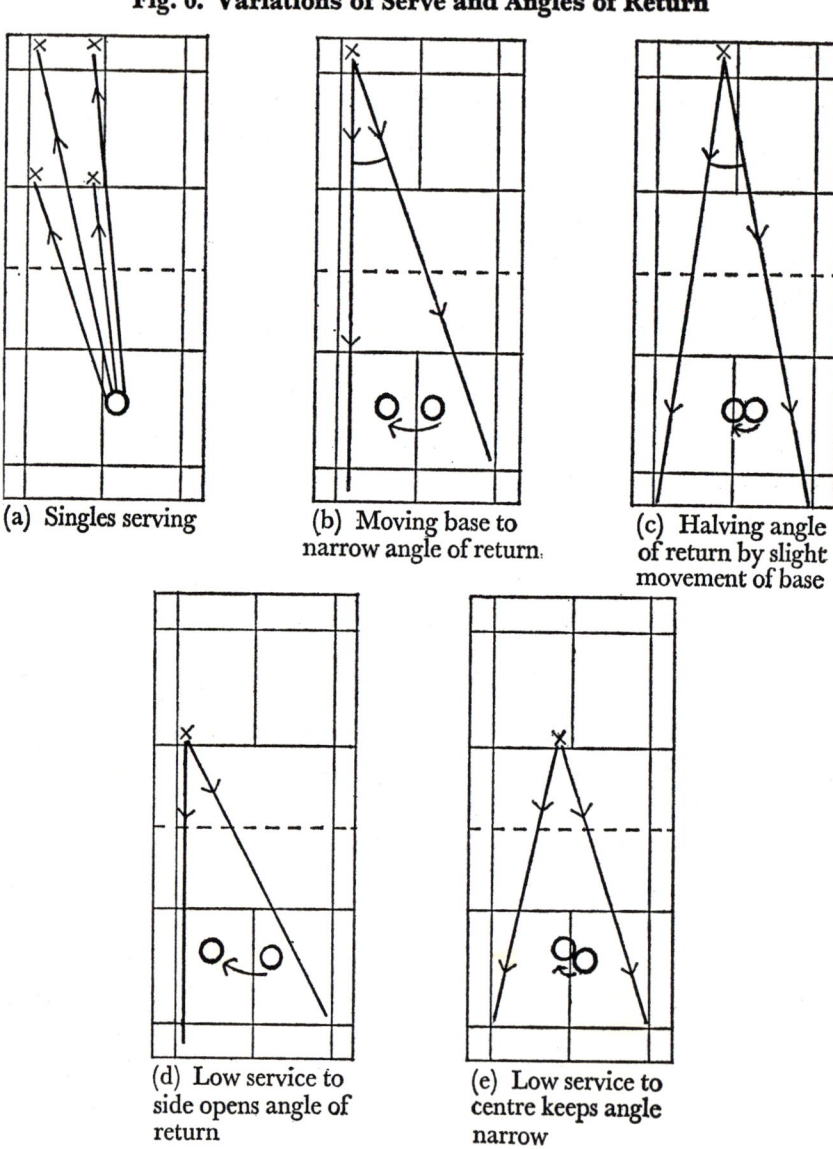

(a) Singles serving

(b) Moving base to narrow angle of return.

(c) Halving angle of return by slight movement of base

(d) Low service to side opens angle of return

(e) Low service to centre keeps angle narrow

position and away from base, play a deep accurate clear to give yourself time to get back. If you are under pressure (i.e. being run around the court) slow the game down by playing high clears. When you have played a lot of singles you learn to anticipate a lot of returns and this anticipation often saves your legs and breath.

When you are attacking allow your opponent as little time as possible to play his shots, smash straight and use cross court only if you see a gap. Smashing to the body cramps the return shot and the use of attacking clears (clears that are low and just clear opponent's racquet) allow less time to run to back line.

Don't get off balance when you smash or you will be slow getting to return shots. Answer accurate drop shots (i.e. those which drop very close to your side of net and which you have to take below the net, near the floor) with high, deep underhand clears to the other back line, but if your opponent is leaving the net vacant then answer with a return net shot, usually called hairpin shot because shuttle flight path takes the shape of a hairpin.

A knowledge of elementary geometry will help your singles and doubles game . . . a knowledge of angles. If you study the angles made when a shot is returned from a particular spot on court, the angle concerned with the flight of the shuttle and the width of the court you will soon appreciate:

(a) When defending you should try to narrow down the angle of return.

(b) When attacking you should have as wide an angle as possible to hit into.

Taking a simple example, when singles serving you should aim at the spot on the back line which will give a narrow angle of return leaving you with a short distance to travel back to a defensive base. A defensive base is the position that gives least danger to either backhand or forehand sides. If you serve from your right-hand court to centre of back line, then step across

47

on to your own centre line, you are giving yourself the best possible chance and most time to meet the danger on either side of you since both angles are equal. The most dangerous shot is the smash to the side lines. If you serve and then stand still you are leaving a wider angle on your left-hand side for your opponent to hit into.

Should you decide to serve to the right-hand forehand corner (the junction of back line and side line), you are leaving a wider angle to hit into—a smash straight down the side lines. To guard against this, when you serve you must step well across centre line to fix your base. A study of the diagrams will help explain this angle of return.

This leads us to another very important question in badminton: cross-courting, or playing the shuttle across the net to the opposite court. This seems a very obvious way to score points, especially to young players. They do it too much, lose points and wonder why, and they usually lose points against the player who thinks.

When used correctly cross-courting is fine but make sure it does not explode against you.

Try to imagine this situation in a game: you are playing a shot from the right-hand side line, your opponent is near his defensive base and you play cross court. You give him a beautiful wide angle to hit into and leave yourself the least possible time to return his shot as the diagram shows. The time to play a cross-court shot is when your opponent is over on one side of the court and well away from his defensive base, then you can plan an angled shot to the other side line. Getting back to geometry, you can work out the possible angles of return from any spot on court and, depending on just where your opponent is, you should learn to play the correct shot at the right time. When caught a long way from base it is a golden rule to play in a straight line—clear into the court straight ahead.

12. Attacking a low serve
13. Playing a clear from the back line
14. Backhand clear

15. Forehand Drive

16. Start of Ladies' Doubles. Both pairs attacking, i.e. back and front

17. Mixed Doubles. Girl in position to play at net

Fig. 7. Cross-courting: Singles and Doubles

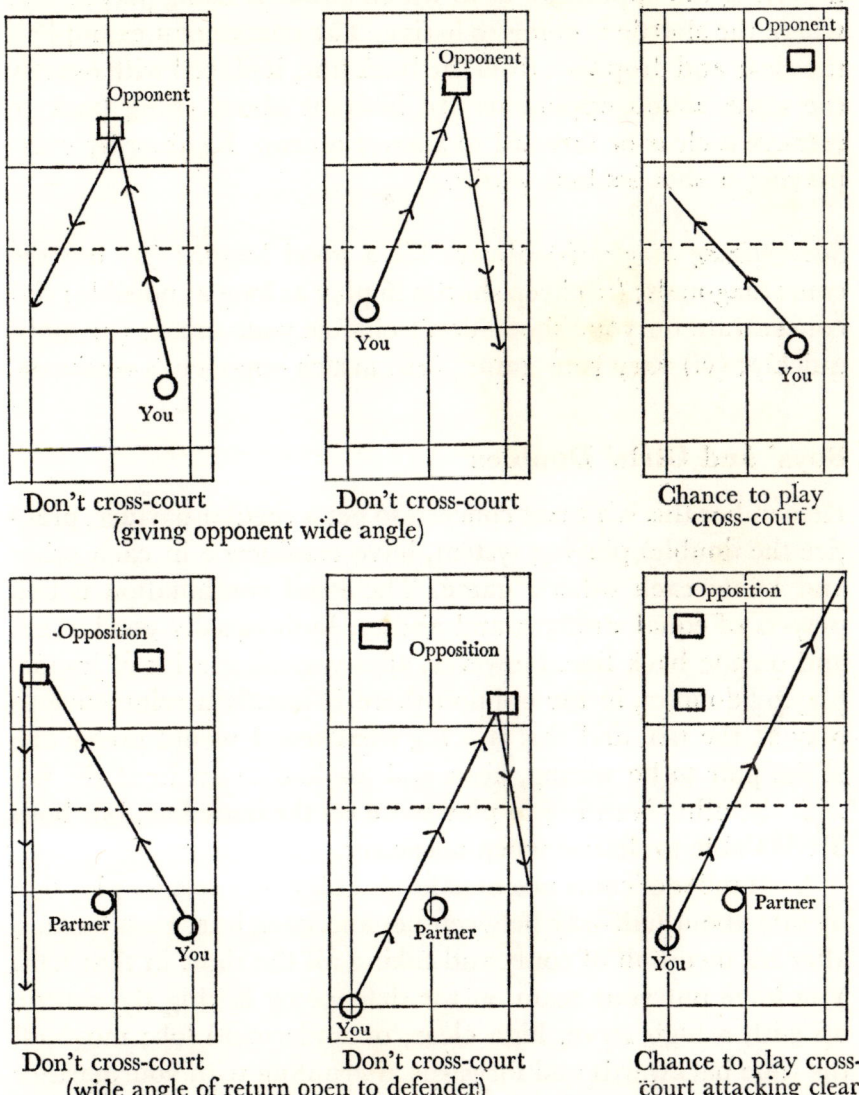

Don't cross-court
(giving opponent wide angle)

Don't cross-court

Chance to play
cross-court

Don't cross-court
(wide angle of return open to defender)

Don't cross-court

Chance to play cross-
court attacking clear

D

Deception is a great help to the singles player: the art of deceiving the opposition as to which stroke is being played and where the shuttle is going to arrive. The commonest example is the clear and drop shot from the back line, if played with exactly the same action opponents are hesitant about going back to retrieve a clear or forward to answer a drop. Kidding by over-playing a shot seldom works.

Summarizing Singles: (i) always hit a good length; (ii) use the court diagonals; (iii) keep shuttle in play as long as possible; (iv) concentrate on your shot—don't change your mind; (v) move quickly; (vi) vary your game; (vii) attack opponent's weakness.

Boys' and Girls' Doubles

Remember this is a team concern so get a regular partner, prac-tice the doubles playing system, have confidence in each other and know each other's game. The ideal combination is two players of equal strength and ability, both equally good at net and on the back line. However, after watching a lot of juniors playing doubles, in my opinion there is usually a reluctance to play at the net, and this is a big weakness. I would prefer one of the pair to be willing, keen and anxious to get in at the net with the other wanting to play more on the back line, but both players able to defend when necessary.

A reminder of court positions for doubles—on defence play side by side about half-way between net and back line, each looking after his own half of court and taking all the shots in that half. You have put your team on the defence by hitting the shuttle up with a high serve, high clear, or underhand lob; move all the time backwards and forwards alternating with your partner until one of you gets the chance to hit down. You are now on the attack again and should take up back and front positions. The main thought in your minds should be to get the attack and keep it.

The low serve is the basic serve in doubles, but be prepared to surprise the opposition by changing speed, direction and even height of service. Keep a narrow angle of return by serving to centre line on inside corner. By serving to opponent's right shoulder you can get a forehand return or a backhand return by aiming for left shoulder (right-handed player), so you will have a good idea where the return is coming to even if attacked; backhand goes to backhand and forehand to forehand. Follow short serve in to net and use flick serve (sparingly) to cool off the receiver constantly rushing you.

When receiving, attack as many low serves as possible, killing the bad ones and pushing the good ones past the receiver to half-court side lines. This forces the back player to take the shuttle low and perhaps put it up. Any high serves should be hit down. Watch the server's wrist and try to spot the flick serve (extra racquet movement and speed is the usual giveaway) and if you do spot it get back and smash; if caught in two minds—clear; if you don't see it you will be up at net, the shuttle will be some way behind you and you will be feeling slightly silly. After serving a flick serve the server goes into net, differing from the high serve when the player drops back to sides.

Some players serve from a position on the outside side lines so they can put the shuttle down to the receiver's backhand. This serve has a surprise value and often gets valuable points, especially if the receiver has a poor backhand or can't smash. On the other hand it leaves more court to be guarded by the server's partner and you do give away your intentions by taking up such an extreme position. The receiver should immediately move back a little to give himself a wider angle and more time to play the shot.

Should you decide to serve high (sometimes necessary to deter

51

an aggressive receiver) keep on altering the angle of serve, sometimes aim for opposite centre line, sometimes forehand corner. Serving to centre line cuts down angle of attack, but if you use other corner your partner should move across behind you to take smash down side lines. Pick up smashes from low backhand and return shuttle to most awkward spot for smasher. Remember you don't have to lift shuttle every time to invite another smash: you can play underhand drop shot to net. Use the cross-court smash with care, remembering it can be turned against you; wait to get defenders close together, or in same court, or when there is an obvious gap left. Drop shots across court are also dangerous—they travel slowly and can be cut off by a fast net player—but they are used, aimed at centre of court at the net to get both defenders there together.

Mixed Doubles

This game causes more arguments in badminton than any other. Many coaches never bother to coach it because they reckon it is on the way out. Many girls hate it because they are often stuck up at the net and only allowed the odd shot in what turns out to be a men's singles game.

There are various schools of thought on how to play mixed doubles: (i) Strictly back and front with the girl at net. (ii) Playing sides in a sort of watered down men's doubles formation but keeping the girl away from back line. (iii) Formation as for men's doubles with man going into net and attacking at every opportunity.

With (ii) and (iii) the girl must be very strong. Since mixed doubles is our best medal winning event in international badminton, it may be as well to carry on the tradition until the singles and other doubles events improve and we can hold our own internationally.

When playing back and front, the tactics are simple. It is an attacking formation, the girl stays at the net and there is no need to change positions. When she serves she moves on to her base on the centre line. Her partner usually serves from behind the girl, from a deeper position than usual, and when serving from left-hand court he may like his partner in front of him in same court. This is to prevent his serve being spoiled and to help cover any weakness on the girl's backhand. Should the man intend to take any net return then he has the girl standing behind him. The main scheme of attack is the half-court shot, the drive, played so that the shuttle falls behind the front service line and to side lines. The idea is to bring the man up to the net and away from back line and at the same time get the lady coming back from the net to help him.

When playing against a 'sides pair' the man of the 'back and front' pair will be run all over the court if he tries to win with smashes and drives only. The 'sides pair' cut the lady out and play to back. The answer should be to force the 'sides pair' away from their bases by playing drop shots, attacking at middle net and driving down the centre of the court.

6

Hints for Advanced Players

When you have achieved proficiency in stroke production and a good knowledge of tactics you require experience in top class competition and a physical fitness programme to keep you in peak condition to carry out heavy playing commitments. There are five Open Junior tournaments in the season and most counties run their own under-18 tournaments. This type of competitive play, along with good individual coaching, will bring out the best in you and help develop your game to the utmost. When playing in good competitive games you must be able to analyse your opponents' game.

Diagnosing Opponents' Game: The E.S.B.A. Award Scheme at Gold Level demands you keep a recorded analysis of a match you have taken part in. A look at their *Observation Game* exam paper will give you an idea what to look for in your opponent's game and your own. You fill in the sheet as soon as you finish and while the games' details are still fresh in your mind. You can also use the sheet to record details of any future opponents: it can be helpful to have a list of future opponents' weaknesses. Here is a sample sheet which I have marked up.

Keeping Fit and Special Training: To be really successful in any sport the player must have a good general standard of

ENGLISH SCHOOLS BADMINTON ASSOCIATION
AWARD SCHEME
Observation Game for Gold Award

Fill in the details as soon as the game is finished. Underline the suggested answer(s) to each section, i.e. the answer you reckon is the best. Should you want to use more than one answer then underline second choice with two lines and third choice with three, etc.

Date *Sat. 12th Dec. 1971* Place *Moorclose Sports Hall* Game *Boys Doubles*

Opponent(s) Name(s) *Jack Latimer George Clarke* Partner's Name *Jim Roxton*

Opponents' Irregularities, e.g. <u>*Left-handed*</u> *Latimer* Small <u>*Tall Clarke*</u>

Opponents' cover of Court	<u>*Good*</u>	*Satisfactory*	*Poor*
Own cover of Court	*Good*	<u>*Satisfactory*</u>	*Poor*
Opponents left most openings	*Net*	*Middle*	<u>*Sides*</u>	*Back*
We left most openings	<u>*Net*</u>	<u>*Middle*</u>	*Sides*	*Back*
Opponents' service was mostly	*High*	<u>*Low*</u>	*Flick*
Our service was mostly	<u>*High*</u>	*Low*	*Flick*
Opponents' return of service mostly	<u>*Rushed*</u>	*Upped*	<u>*Sides*</u>	*Cleared*
Our return of service mostly	*Rushed*	<u>*Upped*</u>	*Sides*	<u>*Cleared*</u>

Opponents lost most points by   <u>*Hitting out*</u>   <u>*Netting*</u>   *Bad tactics*

Superior play of other side

We lost points by   <u>*Hitting out*</u>   *Netting*   <u>*Bad tactics*</u>

<u>*Superior play of other side*</u>

Strength of Opposition *Keeping on the attacking - Smashing - game*

Weakness of Opposition *Careless at times - Latimer slow on back line*

Result of Match *We lost 15/10 15/6*

Strategy to use against same opposition *Keep shuttle down, attack more, and when defending, clear to back line so that we can pick up smashes.*

fitness and to reach that standard, strenuous physical work is required. Your training programme should:

    (a) Build up and maintain a hard core of physical fitness.

    (b) Arrange badminton practices in such a way as to improve your technique and promote fitness.

    (c) Make available special sessions where you play under very strenuous circumstances.

    (d) Provide plenty of competitive play at proper level.

Building up a Hardcore of Fitness: These days a method of training called **Circuit Training** is used to promote and maintain all-round fitness for most sports. This consists of a set number of exercises (circuits) repeated continually and at regular intervals. The load or severity of the exercises is progressively increased, depending on the individual's improvement. This type of training improves the efficiency of the muscular and circulo-respiratory systems, which can be called the engine determining the work output of the body. The better the state of the engine the more work it is capable of without damaging itself. The state of the engine is expressed in **strength** (ability to exert muscular force, e.g. smashing), **muscular endurance** (capacity for continuous heavy activity, e.g. playing lots of clears and smashes), **circulo-respiratory endurance** (stamina, e.g. ability to play long rallies) and **power** (the ability to produce speed and agility, e.g. moving around on a court). The ideal for circuit training is that each performer has a circuit worked out for them and individuals measure their own progress and development. Here is an example worked out for a 15-year-old boy who was training at home where there were no special facilities or apparatus. It lasts about 30 minutes and should be done once a day.

Circuit A

    (1) Continuous *skipping* (like a boxer for 1 minute . . . rest for

30 seconds . . . repeat 5 times. Add 1 extra session each fortnight.

(Purpose: leg strengthening, stamina building and power, agility improvement. This is one of the best general exercises.)

(2) *Wrist rolling:* Use a short wooden bar with cord to which a weight is attached. Weight can be building brick. Unwind and wind continuously for about 5 minutes. Take brick off bar and pass from hand to hand with wrist rolling for another 5 minutes.

(Purpose: grip and wrist strengthening, good for backhand.)

(3) *Chair stepping:* Use a heavy chair about 24–30 inches high. Step up and down on it to 4 count rhythm . . . left up . . . right up . . . left down . . . right down . . . do about 20 steps to minute and keep regular rhythm. Keep going until legs feel weary (about 3 minutes). Add 30 seconds each week.

(Purpose: leg strengthening and stamina building.)

(4) *Trunk curls:* Lie on back, hands resting on thighs. Bend head forward and curl upper part of spine, sliding hands along thighs as far as possible without raising small of back from floor. Do to count of 12. Change to *leg raises* . . . lying with palms on floor, raise both legs to about 12 inches off floor, hold for 3 seconds then lower slowly. Do about 8 times or as many as you are able if you can't make 8. After first fortnight add two more curls and two more leg raises.

(Purpose: abdominal strengthening.)

(5) *Burpees:* Do a continuous four count movement as follows: Stand . . . crouch . . . jump legs back to front support . . . jump legs forward to crouch . . . stand again. Do as many as you can then increase by two each fortnight.

(Purpose: general strengthening, leg and abdominal especially.)

(6) *Dips and presses:* Stand between two strong high-backed chairs put back to back. Hold tops of chairs and support own body weight as if on parallel bars. Bend elbows to right angle while still supporting own weight, if necessary bending knees to keep feet off floor. Work to maximum number of dips then increase by two each fortnight.

(Purpose: arm and shoulder strengthening.)

(7) *Squat jumps:* squat with one foot in front of other. Jump to stretch legs then return to squat with other foot in front. Jump should be as high as possible; work to own capacity and increase by two each fortnight.

(Purpose: leg strengthening and agility exercise.)

Finish off with a burst of continuous skipping or bouncing with feet together. Don't rest between sets of exercises and if you don't feel tired repeat circuit a second time.

Exercises to practise technique and promote fitness: The best way to get fit for badminton is to play badminton, and these exercises combine moving around the court and hitting the shuttle. The best one involves player and coach. The coach stands in the middle of his court and plays the shuttle to all parts of the player's court, making the player move and play shots. The player must hit the shuttle to wherever the coach is standing. There is no question of winning points: the shuttle must be kept going for as long as possible. There is no pressure, the coach making sure the player has time to get to the shot; in fact the player must move and hit in a relaxed manner. The coach dictates the shot he wants in return by his placing of the shuttle and the position he occupies on court. In this way all the shots can be practised, and the player improves his stamina and agility by moving around the court.

Another version can be played between two players deciding which shots to use and working out a rota of shots: drops and clears, underhand lobs and backhand drops, etc. There must be a regular pattern so the player knows exactly where the shuttle is going and where he has to play it to.

Four players may use a court for practice, each pair playing half-court singles, drops and clears.

Playing under specially arranged strenuous circumstances: This is usually known as pressure training and it is a way of improving reaction speed and muscular endurance. The idea is to play certain shots over a long period of time and at high speed until the player becomes tired. Then he goes on playing until he learns to live with the fatigue and bear it. After much pressure training the advent of tiredness comes later and later in the session, or in simple words the player does not get tired so quickly. There are a number of routines which have been worked out such as:

(1) Two players constantly clearing to each other to a certain number.

(2) Two players keep two shuttles going to each other after both serving high together.

(3) Player clears from back line then moves forward to touch front service line with foot or racquet before going back to clear again.

(4) Coach hits high shuttles to various parts of court while player smashes on to a target set on court. About two dozen shuttles needed.

(5) Player smashes from back line at three defenders who lob back.

(6) Player plays against two others, one at net other on back line (one against two). This is good for a singles player who can't get good opposition in his club. It can be

varied to play one against three or four and is a good way of using beginners to help train the better players.

Competitive Play: Unfortunately there are a number of young players who won't enter badminton competitions for various reasons, one obvious one being they won't win it. It is a blow being knocked out in the first round maybe, but a number of tournament organizers now run plate events. All players losing in the first round play in another competition of their own, and you are sure of getting more than one game.

You should look on a tournament as part of your coaching and gaining experience.

The E.S.B.A. in their Award Scheme have competitive conditions at Bronze, Silver and Gold Standards and you cannot get an award unless you have played in a tournament.

Coaching and Coaches: Behind every promising junior player in this country there is probably a coach hidden away. He is somebody who spends a lot of time trying to bring out the best in young players and teaching badminton is usually the least of his troubles. The troubles can vary between arranging practice sessions so as not to interfere with homework—to finding jobs that give time off to play badminton. I have yet to meet a coach who begrudged time given to badminton or who asked for thanks from his pupils. What they do expect is dedication.

If you want to succeed at badminton and you are keen, get regular coaching. Coaching should begin at school and every county schools' association runs its own coaching groups: the progression is from school to district, from district to county, from county to region, and from region to national team. Then somewhere along the line, if you are good enough, the senior county becomes interested, and your progress is watched all the time. There are dozens of school-players playing on senior county teams today.

When you get in a group for coaching don't sit back and expect everything to be done for you, get to all the sessions on time, be willing to take part in all the activities, badminton or P.E., and be prepared to work hard.

7

What Every Young Badminton Player Should Know

Before you take part in any tournament or competition you should be absolutely sure about the rules of badminton and scoring. It is useless blaming your opponent if you don't know when to change ends or when to set and he uses his knowledge to his own advantage. There isn't space to reproduce all the rules here, but you can buy a copy for a small sum at the address given in the next chapter. The Award Scheme of the E.S.B.A. has an oral test on rules of the game for Bronze, Silver and Gold Awards, and the following questions have been taken from the list. If you don't know the answers make it your business to find out and look them up.

E.S.B.A. Oral Questions on Rules. Examiners Select Any Ten

What width should the lines on the court be?

What would be the height of the net at centre?

How would you test a shuttle for correct speed?

Explain the rule about setting in a game of 15 points up.

If you decline to set at 13 all can you set if a score of 14 all is reached later?

In a game of 21 points up when do you change ends?

What Every Young Badminton Player Should Know

If you forget to change ends, can you change when you remember?

The side beginning a game has only one serve in its first innings. True or false?

If during a game you get on the wrong side of the court and the mistake is not discovered for a few services, do you have to change positions and alter the score when you discover your mistake?

Can you stand on the middle line when serving?

If a shuttle falls on the line is it in or out?

If you serve a shuttle through the net is it a fault?

If a shuttle be struck before it crosses the net it is a fault. True or false?

If when serving you miss shuttle completely is it a fault?

What is a sling shot? Can you get a point from it legally?

Is a wood shot legal and what is it?

When serving the racquet should be parallel with the floor. True or false?

If you are not quite ready to receive a service should you try to hit the shuttle?

Both players shall change service courts after each point has been scored. True or false?

The side winning a game should always serve first in next game. True or false?

Should the same order of serving be kept in every game of a match?

Is there any setting in a handicap tournament?

You can leave the court at any time. True or false?

It is perfectly legal to put your racquet up at the net to try and put your opponent off his shot. True or false?

You are allowed to stand on your toes to serve. True or false?

Take your time when you are serving: you can keep your opponent waiting for as long as you like. True or false?

What Every Young Badminton Player Should Know

If you win the toss and give the serve to your opponents you can choose the end you want. True or false?

What is the distance from short service line to net? The length of a doubles court? The width of a singles court?

When serving and receiving in a doubles match all players must stand in their own courts. True or false?

Badminton Literature: I am constantly being asked by young players about books on badminton. Here is a list of titles and authors which will make a good badminton library.

Winning Badminton by Davidson and Gustavon (Anchor Press)

Badminton Complete by P. Davis (Kaye and Ward)

The Badminton Coach by P. Davis (Kaye and Ward)

Better Badminton for All by J. C. Downey (Pelham Books)

Progressive Badminton by K. Crossley (G. Bell)

Teaching Badminton by Gregory and Webb

Modern Badminton by R. J. Mills and E. Butler (Stanley Paul)

Badminton—The Champion's Way by Mrs. J. Devlin Hashman (Kaye and Ward)

18. Men's Doubles.
"Back and Front"
formation

19. Ladies' Doubles.
One pair attacking
(front and back)
One pair defending
(sides)

20. Taking the shuttle early at the net

21. Cumberland and Westmorland Girls Under 16 Team

Left to right: Katherine Fife (English Schools Under 16 and Gold Award)
Janet Fife (Silver Award) Diane Hurst (Gold Award) Shona Stuart (English
Schools Under 16 and Gold Award) Diane and Shona (English Schools Under 16
Ladies Doubles Champions 1971)

8

Opportunity Knocks for Young Players

Although schools' badminton is still in its infancy there is plenty of opportunity for young players of all ages to gain recognition and something worthwhile to aim for.

The E.S.B.A. is made up of affiliated counties including: Cumberland, Lancashire, Essex, Yorkshire, Cheshire, Staffordshire, Shropshire, Isle of Man, Warwickshire, Gloucester, Kent, Middlesex, Herts, Wiltshire, Somerset, Nottinghamshire, Surrey, Westmorland, Worcester, Derbyshire, Sussex, Cornwall and, by the time this book is in print, counties like Berkshire, Devonshire, Oxfordshire, Buckinghamshire, Durham and Hampshire will very likely have affiliated.

Most of these counties run inter-school leagues—boys' teams, girls' teams and mixed teams. Each county has a county team at under-16 level, some under-18, and some under-13, a few run a team for each age group.

There are county tournaments for under-13, under-14, under-15, under-16 and Open Age.

Every season there is a regional match, North v. South v. Midlands, played in Birmingham and the counties in the regions get together for trials to select its best team.

Every year an inter-county championship is organized and counties are invited to send their under-16 teams to play off in a competition similar to the World Cup. In 1972 and 1973 this will be played at Nottingham University along with the Individual Championship. Both competitions run together over three days.

We have annual international games against Scotland and Ireland and plans are afoot to send school international teams to Holland, Denmark, Sweden and Ceylon.

Besides the team events there is the opportunity for every young player to take part in the English Schools Award Scheme and test their badminton ability against certain standards.

E.S.B.A. Award Scheme: The main details are:

Rules: Must belong to a school which is a member of a county schools' association which is a member of E.S.B.A.

Candidates may take the tests at any age and, unless given special permission, in the order of Bronze, Silver, Gold.

There are four parts to each award:
(a) Competitive conditions   (b) Practical
(c) Oral Exam   (d) Written Exam

Bronze Award:

(a) *Competitive conditions:* Candidate must have played for his/her school team and taken part in a schools' tournament organized by the Town, District or County.

(b) *Practical:* Each candidate must satisfy the examiner of his/her technical ability by: Playing a singles match and one doubles match, demonstrating high serve (Singles), low serve (Doubles), high clear and fast drop, and be able to test the speed of a shuttle correctly.

(c) *Oral exam:* Answer ten questions on rules of the game.

(d) *Written exam:* Answer written questions on use of shots and tactics in singles, men's and ladies' doubles and mixed.

Candidates must pass each section of the test and the pass mark is 60 per cent.

Opportunity Knocks for Young Players

In the Bronze Award the total of marks is 100 and approximately 60 are given for practical work.

Examinations for the **Bronze Award** are held very frequently in each county operating the scheme. The examiners are appointed by the counties and are usually B.A. of E. coaches who have kindly volunteered their services.

Silver Award:

(a) *Competitive conditions:* Candidate must have played for the county schools team and taken part in at least one open Junior Tournament.

(b) *Practical:* Play in a singles match, men's and ladies' doubles and mixed. Demonstrate the smash, backhand clear and drop, forehand and backhand drives, and play attacking shots at the net. Umpire a match.

(c) and (d) As for bronze but more difficult written paper.

The full marks total for the silver test is 125, 85 of which are for the practical, pass mark 60 per cent.

The examination for the **Silver Award** is done on a regional basis perhaps two or three times in each season. Each region in the country has a school teacher chief coach for that area and he is responsible for the tests. The coach is usually B.A. of E. County.

Gold Award:

(a) *Competitive conditions:* Candidates must have played for a representative English Schools' Team, or played in North v. South v. Midlands, or played in International trial, or played for a senior county team.

(b) *Practical:* Candidate to play in any doubles/singles match set up by the examiner. Tactical approach will be noted; could be asked to demonstrate a variety of shots; attitude and mental approach when under pressure examined critically.

(c) and (d) As for previous awards but more difficult written paper.

67

(c) Candidate will be required to keep a written record of own game and opponent's game. (Analysis sheet will be supplied.)

The pass mark for the Gold exam is 70 per cent.

The **Gold Award** examination is done nationally and always by the same examiners.

The charge for all tests is 5p and printed cloth badges are available for those who pass the examination, the Bronze and Silver costing 25p, Gold 38p.

The Award Scheme is new and has been running for only the one full season, so far about 150 bronze, 50 silver and 25 gold awards have been made. Many of the gold award winners are junior champions.

Available for anyone and without a test is the E.S.B.A. lapel badge, a brooch type metal one attractively made in the shape of a shuttle, priced 15p.

Cumpstey Cup Winners, 1972:

Glenburn School, Skelmersdale, Lancashire.

A new trophy presented to the Top Badminton School in the country.

Results of Some Important Matches

Results of Some Important E.S.B.A. Matches

Inter-county Championship:

1966	Winners: Cumberland	Runner-up: Lancashire
1967	Winners: Cumberland	Runner-up: Essex
1968	Winners: Essex	Runner-up: Cumberland
1969	Winners: Essex	Runner-up: Surrey
1970	Winners: Lancashire	Runner-up: Nottinghamshire
1971	Winners: Lancashire	Runner-up: Nottinghamshire
1972	Winners: Lancashire	Runner-up: Ulster

Regional Championship

1966	Winners: North	2nd: South	3rd. Midlands
1967	Winners: North	2nd: South	3rd: Midlands
1968	Winners: South	2nd: Midlands	3rd: North
1969	Winners: South	2nd: Midlands	3rd: North
1970	Winners: North	2nd: Midlands	3rd: South
1971	Winners: North	2nd: Home Counties	3rd: Midlands
	4th: South West		

Schools' Individual Championships

1970	Boys' Singles: J. Stretch (Essex)
1971	Boys' Singles: P. Kidger (Yorkshire)
1972	Boys' Singles: P. Wood (Lancashire)
1970	Girls' Singles: N. Gardner (Essex)

Results of Some Important Matches

1971 Girls' Singles: K. Redhead (Lancashire)
1972 Girls' Singles: K. Redhead (Lancashire)
1970 Boys' Doubles: L. Stevens and R. Wallace (Warwick.)
1971 Boys' Doubles: A. Fish and I. Loten (Nottinghamshire)
1972 Boys' Doubles: P. Wood and G. Scott (Lancashire)
1970 Girls' Doubles: N. Gardener and C. Beer (Essex)
1971 Girls' Doubles: S. Stuart and D. Hurst (Cumberland)
1972 Girls' Doubles: G. Scholey and C. Kelly (Lancashire)
1970 Mixed Doubles: T. Wing and C. Salmon
                                    (Nottinghamshire)
1971 Mixed Doubles: G. Roberts and A. Gardner (Surrey)
1972 Mixed Doubles: P. Littlewood and P. Mason
                                    (Lancashire)

International Matches

1968 English Schools Under-16 defeated Scottish Schools Open Age

1969 English Schools Under-16 lost to Scottish Schools Open Age

1969 English Schools Under-16 defeated a Danish Junior Team

1970 English Schools Under-16 drew with Scottish Schools Open Age

1971 English Schools Under-16 drew with Scottish Schools Open Age

1971 English Schools Under-16 defeated Irish Schools Under-16

1972 English Schools Under-16 drew with Scottish Schools Open Age

1972 English Schools Under-16 defeated Irish Schools Open Age

Some Very Useful Addresses

Hon. Secretary, Badminton Association of England:
J. B. H. Bisseker, Esq., 81 High Street, Bromley, Kent, BR1 1JY.

Hon. Secretary, English Schools Badminton Association:
L. Wright, Esq., 5 Starnthwaite, Crosthwaite, Kendal, Westmorland.

Coaching Secretary, B.A. of E.:
(Use this address for copy of rules and information about coaching courses.)
Mrs. O. Johnson, 3 Sunnyside Road, Ealing, London, W.5.

Regional Coaches, E.S.B.A.:
North: A. Horrocks, Esq., 4 Spring Street, Oswaldtwistle, Accrington, Lancs, BB5 3EW.

Midlands: N. R. J. MacFarlane, Esq., 134 Norton Lane, Tidbury Green, Wythall, Warwickshire.

South: F. New, Esq., 7 Upper Park, Harlow, Essex.

Any details concerning the Award Scheme can be obtained from Hon. Sec. English Schools, but the following teachers are operating in their own areas:

Cumberland: I. Graham, Esq., 22 Sneakyeat Road, Hensingham, Whitehaven.

Lancashire: K. Smith, Esq., 5 Woodrow Drive, Newburgh, Parbold, Wigan.

Yorkshire: J. Monkman, Esq., 22 Rosamond Avenue, Sheffield, S17 4LT
H. Jarvis, Esq., 15 The Causeway, Thorpe Willoughby, Selby.

71

Some Very Useful Addresses

Essex: H. A. Napier, Esq., 43 The Drive, Cranbrook, Ilford.

Nottinghamshire: S. Robinson, Esq., Low Street, Newark, Nottinghamshire.

Staffordshire: E. A. Winter, Esq., 178 Whetstone Lane, Aldridge.

Somerset: J. I. Davis, Esq., 9 Southfield Close, Taunton.

Warwickshire: N. R. J. MacFarlane (address above).

President E.S.B.A. and Chairman B.A. of E. Coaching Committee: P. A. Johnson, Esq., 3 Sunnyside Road, Ealing, London W.5.